from sand to stars

shelby leigh

central
avenue

2024

This is a work of fiction. Names, characters, places and incidents either are the
product of the author's imagination or are used fictitiously and any resemblance to
actual persons, living or dead, business establishments, events or locales is entirely
coincidental.

Published by Central Avenue Publishing, an imprint of Central Avenue Marketing Ltd.
www.centralavenuepublishing.com

FROM SAND TO STARS

Trade Paperback: 978-1-77168-388-3
Epub: 978-1-77168-389-0

Published in Canada
Printed in United States of America

1. POETRY / Women Authors   2. POETRY / General

10 9 8 7 6 5 4 3 2 1

for those who fear they are running out of time
to find themselves, love themselves, be themselves

a note to my readers

in two of my poetry books, *changing with the tides* and *girl made of glass*, I wrote my poems with a lowercase i which, at the time, represented the smallness I felt as I struggled with my self-esteem. I viewed myself as small, so *i* became small.

as time goes on (which, spoiler alert, is a big theme of this book!), I no longer identify with that small i. in *from sand to stars*, you'll find that although there are days I still struggle, as you might as well, I will no longer be making myself small.

this change may feel small, but to me, it represents hope, growth, and the work I've put into realizing my worthiness.

I hope it helps inspire you to take up space, too.

Sand

time & tension

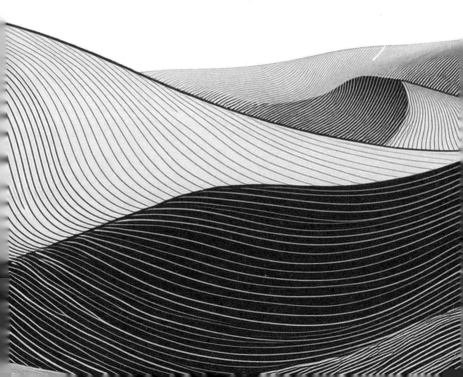

watch how quickly sand
falls in the hourglass.
>*I can't escape the irony of my thoughts—*
>*wasting time worrying about not having enough time.*
I count the days, weeks, months
since I achieved something significant.
I do not want to be just a checkmark on a to-do list,
no, I desire a dent in the core of the earth,
a stamped footprint that never lifts.
it feels like centuries since I've felt worthy of taking up space.
I remind myself that even a century is small
in the existence of the entire world.

and some days like today,
it feels good to feel small.
to remember that I have so much time
to achieve big things.

and when time disappears
I want to believe in slowness again.

I want to believe that my heart does
not have to race to feel alive,

that I do not have to pump my
arms and run in my sleep to win

the marathon against my mind.
I want to believe there is a finish

line my legs will reach,
that on the other side I can sit

in the quiet and close my eyes
without feeling like I'm sitting in

wasted time. can I live in a world
that isn't constantly spinning?

maybe then I won't feel like I always
have to be moving, running, leaping.

let stillness sit with you.
let silence seep in, too.
and when serenity says *hello*,
savor it.

sometimes I fear I'm not really living but
I don't know how to break my routine.
I'm scared things won't return to normal but
I'm not even sure what normal means.
maybe normalcy isn't something to wish for but
rather something to fear.
maybe if life were the same each day,
I wouldn't know which moments to hold dear.

when I hear her, she is bold, loud. everyone turns to look at her and she loves it—the attention. I squint my eyes and feel my throat dry. in this story, she is me, a version I don't recognize, living in an alternate universe where I am someone worth talking to, worth getting to know. I shut my eyes, scream internally, try to make noise, try to be noticed in this life. here.

somewhere, in an alternate universe, there is a version of me who doesn't feel alone.

wishful thinking:

sometime in the future I won't feel alone.
somewhere there is a girl just like me who is happy.
somehow I will be happy, too.

what's your biggest fear?

that I'll never know if I am
truly happy,
or just content.

that I'll always wonder
if there was more for me
than the life I lived.

I don't know how to be alone
without feeling alone. I used to know
how to be happy,
or at least content, on my own.
but lately when I'm by myself,
all I do is overthink,
spend hours staring at the ceiling
while my mind replays moments
I thought I left behind.

when I think of all my yesterdays,
        I think they are cruel—
because of me.
because I wished them away hoping
for a better tomorrow.
I felt rain and wished for sunshine.
I cried and wished for laughter.

when I think of all my ghosts
stuck in all of my yesterdays,
        I'd like to think they are happy.
I'd like to think
they are splashing in the rain,
living for today
instead of praying for tomorrow.

I try to clear out the cobwebs in my mind, take a broom to my brain and shake out all my sins. my head has always hung heavy, eyes to the ground, neck to navel. I can't shake the cobwebs and I can't shake the feeling that I'd be better off letting them take over. letting the creepy crawly things build a home in my brain so I can't live here anymore.

I'm so glad my body can still be used as a home for something, *anything*. because I don't use it as a home for me.

my mind spins and it feels inhuman, like I'm chasing something that can't be drowned, that keeps coming back to the surface, that stays alive no matter how hard I try to push it down. the negative thoughts sink below the surface and I think I'm finally free, but when I look at the water, there they are, staring back at me.

home can be created, built outside of you.
but I hope you'll find home in your body, too.

can you lose yourself
if you never really knew
who you were?

can you find yourself
if you never really knew
who you were?

the sand in my chest
builds with every breath.

I swallow the ocean to find air,
to rise.

but instead, I sink.
the entire ocean

is too heavy to hold.
I'm drowning but

I dream of victory,
of smiling despite the pain,

of no one knowing
all that I carry.

what light you bring to the world
while you carry darkness.

when the darkness sits over
my head like a storm cloud,
I search for light wherever I can
find it.
sometimes I find it in the
reflections of the raindrops
that dance on my skin.
sometimes I find it in the
moonlight.

sometimes I cannot find
the light at all,
so I wait.

my palms forget the calm,
the steady rhythm when I press
them to my chest.
my heart beats like rain during a
storm. hurtling toward the ground.
pounding against pavement.

my lungs forget the deepness.
the calm breaths that
fill my chest full.
and my mind—
oh, how it forgets to slow.
always running to escape the rain,

never stopping to notice the clouds.
how they glide so peacefully
even in the midst of a downpour.
how they part to make room for a rainbow.
how they wait for the
calmness and beauty
after the storm.

the rain keeps me up
another night.
every thought in my head
is a heavy raindrop knocking
on the window.
it yells, *I'll never let you forget.*
my eyes are squeezed shut,
pillow pressed to the sides of
my head, but nothing
works. the rain knocks and
knocks until I fall asleep
finally
and then

the rain enters my dreams.

at night,
my mind says,
I'll never let you forget.
I'll never let you forget.
I'll never let you forget.
I'll never let you forget.
I'll never let you forget.
I'll never let you forget.
I'll never let you forget.

I have never known
silence.
my mind is always
loud.
a tornado of words
swirling around my head.

I cannot escape
the noise.

and for my next trick, anxiety doesn't live here anymore

she packed her bags—no, I packed them for her and kicked her out. and somehow I feel emptier, like all my oxygen has been siphoned from my body, like I don't know how to be if I am not filled with doubt, with anger, with regret. it is a mystery, how she waves her magic wand and comes back into my life. because even when she moved out of my mind, she entered my body, my soul. she's never leaving, never ending, never fearing. I want her gone. why won't she go?

if my brain let me, I would step on ants just because. press the heel of my shoe into the floor and count to three. I would lift my foot and not feel a thing. take a tissue to the tile and toss it in the trash. if my brain let me, I would scream at the top of my lungs. close my eyes and let out every drop of disappointment that has ever entered me without permission. declare war on my windows, shatter the glass and never sweep up the pieces.

if my brain let me, I would get through the day without thinking about you in present tense, as if there's a chance you'll walk through my dead-bolted door. as if there's a chance you'll ever leave my mind.

some days I sink into the feeling of loneliness, search for hidden memories in between couch cushions, fan my hands over trodden carpet for souvenirs of my past. some days I put headphones in and scroll through my music library, as if it's there I will find the sound of your voice. as if there you have been waiting all along.

you don't know me anymore
and I'm okay with that.

on any given morning,
you can find me half alive.
heavy steps across the carpet,
ankle weights sewn to my legs.
eyes too weary to widen.
I pinch my skin,
watch my flesh whiten under the pressure,
pull my hair hard enough that my neck bends—
nothing.
alive, yes,
but not how I want to be.

I stand with my legs split on two paths and my eyes torn in different directions. I know the way my heart is pulling me, and I know the way my mind is telling me to go. the smart way, the safe way, the way that will protect me, the way that makes my heart beat slowly. but is that the life I want? always certain? never unknowing?

I don't want to be dust on a mantel, nor a body in the ground. I want to be a pen of ink, a blue jay that knows no bounds, the creak in a chair that has been loved for generations. a scuff on the floor where children play. crayon on a white wall, handprint in dried cement. something to prove I lived a life. something remembered and loved.

as I jump into the river at el yunque rainforest, I feel the weight of my body lighten, even as I sink. in the four seconds of flying before I hit the water, I had plenty of time to think about what was below me. dark water, slithering eels, a hand to drag me down. I pushed myself off the edge before anxiety tied my feet to the ground, but she still turned up in those four seconds. but by then, it was too late to go back to land. by then, I had felt the thrill, the lightened body. when I came up from dark water, and took my first coughing breath, I left her there. I let her sink. and climbed back up the cliffside so I could push myself free once more.

some days I walk to the creek
just to look at myself in the water's reflection
like some kind of narcissist,
but really, I like the haziness of my face
in moving water.
it's harder to see the flaws.

poem beginning with a retweet
after maggie smith

if you see this, retweet with a photo of you smiling.
so I scroll through my photo gallery,
back to january, now september, now march.
and I can't find a single one. I don't take
pictures like I used to. at least not of myself.
when I was young, it was so easy for me to
put on a smile and share it on my screen.
but in the blink of an eye,
I learned what beauty means,
so my smiles came less and less.
and now it's been
months since I've taken a picture of myself.
months since I've tinted my lips
and stepped in front of my window
for bright lighting that flatters me best.
tell me, should I put on a smile today
so I can fit into a twitter trend?
or will everyone see through my deception?

anti-aging

what a privilege it is to grow old.
to wear lines on your face that
memorialize every emotion you've experienced,
to live a life so colorful you've
left a rainbow in your path,
left your hair gray and white.

I am pro-aging.
I want the lines of my life written on my body.

so, let me get this straight.
we spend our formative years being sold
lip plumper, lash lifts, and liposuction.
and then, by the time we start to like our bodies,
and realize everything we'd been told is wrong,
we're handed hair dye and wrinkle cream and stretch mark serum
because we aren't supposed to like our bodies . . . ever?
not when we're young; not as years pass.

so, when?

when will I be
allowed to love
my body as it is?

I look back at the shadow of my life and sit in it. a wave of darkness, I can barely make out my own two hands in front of me. it is cold here, even though much of my life I thought was warm. and still, one shadow can send me down into a hole I dug myself. when I can finally see my hands again, they are dirt-covered and sore, evidence of my own destruction. I look up, spot a ray of sun casting light on the ground and step into it. a reminder that I don't have to live in the shadows I create. a reminder that there is light if I can just escape.

I take turns with grief, like we're two friends playing on a seesaw at the park. one moment, grief lifts me up, envelops me in sunlight, and the next moment I hit the ground, feeling the earth shake beneath me. we do everything together, grief and I—sit at the dinner table, slice silence with a steak knife, leave half-eaten memories on our plates.

in the evenings, we lie on the couch together and fill the room with laughter from the tv. ever since I became friends with grief, laughter hasn't come from me.

you have time.
you will grow and
build confidence and
change paths and
make mistakes and
love deeply and
find new passions and
laugh freely and
cry from joy and
cry from pain and
isn't it so beautiful

how much we get to feel?

we try so hard to
forget the ugly parts
of life,
but without them,
how would we know
what is beautiful?

repeat after me:

I am not running out of time—
I am running toward something great.
I am not wasting time—
I am chasing what I know will bring me joy.

I am small in this universe,
but my impact will be big.

you don't have to have it all figured out,
today or in a month or in a year.
and when you *do* figure it out,
then you can figure it out again.
you can change your mind,
change your passion,
learn something new,
let something go.
there is no right age to finalize your life.
there is no timeline on your happiness.
life is not one puzzle to solve—
it is endless pieces that fit together perfectly
some days
and not the next.
it is making mistakes and learning that it
was exactly what needed to happen to
find your next path.

you don't need to walk along
anyone else's path.
knock down the wall,
trample on the grass,
turn left instead of right.

your life is yours.

Soil
growth & guidance

my garden is empty, dead. I forgot to water it.
I fill up my watering can and set it to the side.
good intentions, sure, but not enough
to keep flowers blooming.
my garden is empty, barren.
I walk through it over and over,
rush too much and crush
petals beneath my feet.
my garden is empty,
colorless. where flowers once grew,
lie brown and broken stems.

I know you're disappointed. you thought you were getting better, but lately, you feel hopeless, right back where you never wanted to be. and you promised yourself you would never be here again.

I'm so sorry for this hurt, but I want you to know progress has still been made. and even though there will be more days like this, too—I'm proud of you.

there are ups and downs.
there are small steps forward and giant steps back.
but every day, no matter how disappointed you feel,
remember—there is no one right way to heal.

I thought I was brave for leaving, but I didn't realize the hold you had on me when I left. you kept the unfamiliar parts of me that I forgot even existed. the parts that took me being alone to miss.

the broken parts of me wanted
the whole parts of you.

I wanted someone to prove to me
that I could be whole again, too.

I don't find myself
missing you anymore.

now I just miss me,
the one I used to be.

you painted me on a canvas
and hung it in the sky.
you tried to change my colors,
but the paint had already dried.
you wanted me to be what I'm not,
someone completely new.
but if I ever change myself,
it will be for me—not you.

the plants I've killed have been
under-watered.
under-loved.
I do not have a heavy hand.
I do not pour my heart out.

it is not lost on me that the relationships
I've killed have been
under-watered.
under-loved.
I'm so afraid of giving too much
that I just don't give at all.

I loved you far before I ever loved me.
and that's okay. I wasn't ready.
you tried to help me, and in the end, it wasn't our time.
it had to end because I was giving you every ounce of love
I had and leaving myself with nothing.
it had to end. but thank you for showing me
that I could love.

because I loved you,
I know I can love myself, too.

it is easy to say *I love you*. it isn't easy to put in the work to understand what makes someone tick. what keeps them up at night, the fire that glows in their heart. tell me something real. show me that you *know* me.

you ebbed and flowed
like waves in the sapphire sea,
flooding me with love and
then leaving me be.

you came and went
like leaves on autumn trees.
when I thought we were growing close,
you fell further from me.

I know you thought I couldn't cope,
that without you I'd never get by,
but now that you're gone from my life—
now I can finally thrive.

when I think of flowers, I think of rain.
how it destroys, how it heals.
when I think of destruction I think of you.
but when I think of healing I think of me.
how you tried so hard to drown me.
how I stayed above water anyway.

something I wished I had told you:
maybe you had closure, but I didn't.

maybe you'll never read this,
but it's still the ending I need.
let me pour my heart into the hands
that were always closed:

I tried to love you as much as I knew how.
there comes a time when a person
can no longer act as an atm,
a piggy bank,
slipping love in like coins whenever you'd allow.
little pieces of me went with them,

and you kindly kept them all.
it may not seem like I've moved
on as I write this poem, but I have.
maybe you're hoping that this will
end in forgiveness, but it doesn't.
it ends with me,

reclaiming all the love I gave to you.
it has always been mine.

one of the hardest lessons I've had to learn is
that beautiful things come to an end, too—
rainbows,
sunny days,
walks in the park,
a life with you.

she doesn't *need* anyone but herself,
but it's not wrong that she *wants* someone.

she can be independent and still receive love.
she can be independent and still give love.

you're a giving person,
and that's beautiful.
but be sure to listen to
your body.
giving people should
give to themselves, too.

at some point, you must
stop chasing the ones who hurt you.
allow yourself to catch your breath,
then turn around and
run back to yourself.

pretend your body is a garden,
a field of flowers
that needs water
and sunlight
and love to grow.

and your mind is its keeper,
put in charge of caring
for every beautiful part of you.

some days,
you will forget to water,
nurture, love.

give yourself grace
on those dehydrated days.

I loved the idea of loving you
and hated the idea of losing you.

so I poured everything I had
into you until I was exhausted and empty.
and then you left.
and that's okay.

I thought I hated the idea of losing you.
but it turns out I really love the idea of loving me.

in fall, I am given a chance to start fresh.
I rake up all my self-pity, stuff it in a plastic bag,
and drag it to the curb.
I can breathe,
with everything I've been carrying now lifted from me.

I stretch my arms above and smile briefly before winter comes,
dumping the bitter heaviness right back on my shoulders.
brush it off. get back up.
I do it every time.

I always do what I've been told.

but autumn keeps getting shorter;
the bright days come and go.
I can't help but wonder—

what if, even though I've survived every dark winter
and shown up ready for spring,
the light doesn't show up for me?

I once carried the weight of other people, let them attach their words to me like weights. I dragged my feet through each day, walking slower and slower, never getting where I needed to be. with no end in sight, I fell to my knees, ashamed that I couldn't make it any further. my heart pounded and my arms burned as I lifted weight after weight from my body. my feet began to lift from the ground and I was floating.

all along I was meant to be floating.

wintertime always reminds me of what matters.
the things that bring warmth to my life.
the people I search for when I'm cold
and the places I go when I need light.

there's something beautiful
about houseplants going dormant
in the winter,
protecting their energy
for when the warmth
and light come back,
saving their strength
so they can live to
see another spring.

if you are feeling empty,
bare your roots to the sky
and let the rain plant you
like a seed,
reborn into a new flower.

you may not be perfect,
but then again,
who wouldn't want a beautiful flower
just because it had
a missing petal,
a bent stem?

learning to be loud comes with many half-spoken sentences, soft mutters and blushing cheeks. learning to be loud means cutting through can'ts, slicing through stops, and resisting the rejection your mind recites on replay. when you learn to be loud, others will prefer when you were quiet. they will prefer when you let them do all the talking. when you are loud, your mind will tell you to turn down the volume. but once you learn to be loud, the earth will welcome your voice. it will carry you across valleys and echo you up mountainsides. once you learn to be loud, you will wonder how you were ever quiet.

when I get to my parents' house and bring my bag
up to my childhood bedroom, the still-purple walls
wrap me in a hug. immediate safety beyond the wood door.
the room says, *welcome back*,
and I don't have the heart to tell those four walls
that I am not the girl they once knew—
the girl who lay in this bed with a stack of books
on the weekends, the girl who stood in front of the
mirror and hoped for her reflection to change.
I am not the girl who preferred being nameless, invisible.

I don't say any of that.
I don't have the heart to say,
you don't know me anymore.
because one day, these purple walls will be painted over,
and I won't recognize them anymore either.

but no matter how many layers are added,
their true colors will still be there.

I am still me,
but I have grown
and changed
and learned.
you may not recognize me anymore,
but I am living life
like I've always wanted.

every day, unintentionally,
I find a little more of me.
something to love,
something to learn to love,
something to enthrall myself in for weeks.

every day, unintentionally,
I find something new to appreciate.
the taste of a new recipe,
the wind on my skin,
an old poem I never finished.

every day, unintentionally,
I find that the world changes colors.
some days it is black-and-white.
some days it is filled with color.

every day, *intentionally*,
I find a reason to be
happy I'm alive.

she peered inside a dark wishing well, could barely see shiny coins 100 feet below. she had been told of this well, that anything she wished would come true. so there she walked, each and every day, pulling a coin from her pocket and tossing it down.

"I wish to be beautiful."

"I wish to be noticed."

"I wish he would love me."

she heard every coin hit the water below, though she couldn't see them fall, and every day for years she came, dropped a coin and made a wish. each coin, along with rainwater, filled the well higher and higher until one day, the woman bent over and saw her reflection just a couple of feet below her face. and in her reflection, she was surprised to see wrinkle lines and graying hair. it had been years since she saw her reflection, and for the first time in a long time, she smiled, remembering her first wish: to be beautiful. and she was, all along.

but this time, she saw it herself.

1. the cold sinks into my hair and I'd barely recognize me even if my reflection crept by in the street. red cheeks, eyes to ground, hands in pockets. all hope is not lost but I have lost some.

2. flowers bloom and I try to emulate their form. lift my head inch by inch like a plant that's just been watered. the sun pulls its rays gently through my hair. all hope is not lost. in spring, I found some.

3. summer reminds me of days at the pool, towel flung to the ground as I jump in and spread my wings. now my arms wrap around my body, protecting me from the things I imagine people say. I pretend I am giving myself a hug. all hope is not lost, but god, I hope for more.

4. colors change year after year and this time I do, too. my reflection smiles at me as she walks by. all hope is not lost.

I searched for hope in the sea
but she was nowhere around me.

I climbed mountains to see far
but she wasn't in the stars.

I looked within
and there she was, hidden.

I see you,
closed off to love,
hands crossed over your chest.

I see you,
averted eyes in the mirror,
hope clung to your sleeve—
tugging for attention.

it's there for you when you need.

in the quiet of the morning,
under the bridge,
hidden away in a forest of spruce trees,
is a path not so easy to find.
after a rainy day, you won't
often see footprints in the mud,
but tucked away is a single picnic table,
rotted at both ends of the bench
where I often sit and listen.

in the quiet of the morning,
the moon is still awake,
the birds do not yet sing,
and the wind softly howls as it steps closer.
I must fill the silence, I decide, not
with singing or howling, but with music.
so I sit cross-legged on a damp wooden bench,
open my notebook,
hold my pen and
watch the wind dance
it around the pages,
to the music in my head.

in the quiet of the morning,
I do not wish for anyone
to fill the silence.
for once, I sit with myself instead.

don't let anyone tell you that self-love is a linear journey. that once you find acceptance for yourself, there will never be a day of doubt again. don't believe that you are alone in your battle, that others aren't facing the same obstacles as you. (even if the armor they're wearing looks different.) don't believe there's a fast fix to finding yourself, loving yourself, accepting yourself. believe that you will find yourself, love yourself, accept yourself. no matter how long it takes.

I walked to the corner store
when the sun was setting
and my shadow walked with me
along the way,
and as I looked at the pavement,
watched her legs keep pace with mine,
my fears dissolved and I realized we are not enemies.

myself and I are two friends walking side by side.

it took a sacrifice to learn to love myself.
I had to give away all the hatred
I had been lugging on my back.

harder than it sounds—
to abandon something
you have known your whole life.

it was a gradual process,
like sand delicately falling in an hourglass,
piece by piece.

Stars
hope & healing

I've never found hands big enough
to hold the love I have to give.
all along I've placed my heart into
others' palms and watched it fall to the ground.
so I picked up the pieces,
tried again and again to mold my soul
so it would fit where I (thought I) needed it to be.

all along I've been giving away this love and
all along I never noticed my own empty hands.
all along they have been open,
            palms to the sky,
waiting.

when the sky opens, it is like magic. it is like everything I ever wanted is here with me now. I never thought I would see this day or trust in my life enough to live it, to open my arms to the sky and let rain pour from my eyes. it is such a wonder to know this life. such a wonder to know that I have happier days ahead.

how lucky are we to be alive?

the stars dance in the light of the moon
and I watch them closely,
twinkling and twirling to the music—
crickets chirping,
wind whistling.
the stars in the sky
lift me from the heaviness.
they remind me that I can dance
with no music and no one around.
they remind me that even in a vast sky,
the tiniest shimmers of light
make a big impact.

our minds are a map of everything we've been through and sometimes we lose our way. whether we are misguided by people we trust, who take us down the wrong path, or we get lost on our own, there will always be a way back. don't blame yourself for getting lost—this is your chance to journey somewhere new.

you are being pulled
in two different directions,
like fabric on a clothing line,
pulled by the wind.

here, you are safe, comfortable, home.
but what if you let go,
and the wind took you
somewhere new, unexplored?
what if, in this new place,
you finally felt free?

we are not the sun,
returning to the same point in the sky,
year after year.

we are growing,
blooming,
healing,
wishing,
hoping,
breathing,

being.

the point in the sky
directly above you is called
zenith.
it is yours and yours alone—
only you are in this spot
in this moment
in time.

the next time you feel unworthy,
remember the little piece of sky
you carry on your shoulders.

carry it proudly, wherever you go.

someday you'll find the one meant to make you smile, laugh, feel safe.
the one meant to lift you up. you'll be looking for that person in others,
everywhere you turn. and then, one day, you'll find them in the reflection
of your mirror, the trembling hand pressed to your chest, the shaky breath
that reminds you how fast your heart beats.

where I live, the cracks in the road are covered every spring. but come winter, the cold breaks the concrete, and we drive over divots, the cars jostling up and down.

even when we try to heal, the cracks are not far below. even when we pretend we're okay, the cracks still show.

tell me:
do you know how brilliant you are?
are you going to live this one life
not believing in the one heart that
has beat every second of your life?
the mind that has made your every good decision?
the soul that believes in you under all the doubt?
the one person who will be with you
for every moment of your one brilliant life?

I can see it—every mistake you've made is sitting heavy on your chest. close your eyes. put your palms to your heart and feel the magnitude of its beating. pulsing through your body. take a deep breath and feel your heart slow.

you cannot take back your mistakes. they happened. you cannot take back the times you've doubted yourself. they happened. but you can lift the weight from

your body.
your body—

it's tired.

it needs room to breathe. lift your hands up to the sky, push all of the regrets and worries and doubt away. feel how high your chest can rise now, without the weight holding it down.

watch it all float away.
it's a new day.

body:

I regret not loving you sooner,
~~but I do now.~~
but I'm trying.
thank you for not
giving up on me.

mind:

you've put me through
a *lot*. I know you were
just trying to protect
me. you have so many
beautiful, kind, creative
thoughts. you have so
many anxious, critical
thoughts. I love you
all the same.

a reminder to slow down.
a reminder to breathe.
a reminder that you are exactly where you need to be.

the minutes will continue to pass you by. you'll live and breathe and smile and sigh and stress, and some moments will pass you by while others will be memories etched in time. hold on to the moments you never want to forget. take the picture. write in the journal. tell the stories, no matter how many times you've told them before. don't let the memories fade.

remember that rest is productive, too. a day on the couch is a day well spent if your body and mind have asked you for it.

I dreamt I was a cloud floating through the air,
taking myself wherever I needed to be.
people can act like the wind and help me along,
but no one can shape my life except me.

my heart is healing
and I'm opening
myself up to be loved
and appreciated.

I know that I could still get hurt,
but I could also be really happy.

my body runs on creativity.
with every new idea,
my mind is off to the races,
thinking of all the possibilities,
the new world we'll create.

tell me—
what makes your mind soar?
your stomach flip with joy?
if you haven't found it yet,
please don't give up your search.

please don't come back to your dreams at a "better" time. starting now, when you're busy and stressed, will still put you further ahead than if you start five years from now (when you will still be busy and stressed). we like to think there will be a perfect time to start, that the stars will align and the opportunity will fall into place, but the opportunity is already here, waiting. take it.

I don't know what tomorrow holds
but I do know today is already here.
right in front of you.
what will you do with it?

please hold on to your hope.
don't let it slip away.

how are you? no, really. don't just say, *I'm fine.* how are you? when was the last time you asked yourself, *how am I?* your shoulders are tense, your eyes need rest, and your mind is juggling so much. I hope you know it's okay to put down everything you're carrying. give your back a break. close your eyes, just for a moment.

I watch a mother hold up an oval mirror to entertain her infant son.
his eyes widen at his own reflection, reaching toward the cold glass and
squishing his hand against it, taking in his own big beautiful eyes, his
mouth open in fascination. for this moment, I am okay with mirrors. how
a child can look at his reflection and see everything beautiful about the
world, about himself. and if the world were perfect, it would stay this way.
no child would be told they need to look a certain way. no child would one
day look in the mirror and see every little thing they hope will change. they
wouldn't begin to hate their reflection. they wouldn't wish, as I some days
do, that mirrors didn't exist. but for this moment, I am okay with mirrors.
it is worth it to see a child so in love with their own reflection.

joy is:

feeling at home in my body / closing my eyes after a long day / tasting the first cookie out of the oven / getting a hug from someone I've really missed / laughing until my belly is sore / writing with a pen full of ink / listening to someone I love talk about what makes them happy

I danced freely at age 11—
leaps across the kitchen floor,
pirouettes in front of the mirror.

I took a magnifying glass to my face at 13,
zoomed in on my skin—
pink craters and tiny hills. I loved
nature before I saw in my face
a mountain,
all the obstacles I had to climb.

past the sharp edges on a cliff,
my mind bravely took a dive
but did not land on its feet.
at 15, I took a bow that never lifted,
shoulders curled forward,
forehead to floor.

by 16, I mastered the smile—
slight curl, lips pressed.
when 17 came, I was a ghost,
proudly afloat.
no eyes looked at me—
I was okay with that.
danced in my head
but never my body.

18 came and for the first time
I wanted to be noticed, and
at 19, I learned
that being loved
wasn't enough.

at 20, I was on my own—
this time,
I didn't feel alone.

I took a magnifying glass
to my passions and interests at 21,
explored life instead of my flaws,
lifted my bow so
the world could see me stand tall.

I dance freely at 26—
leaps across the kitchen floor,
pirouettes in front of the mirror.

(it gets better.)

I'm sorry
for all the years
I didn't let you fly.

my shadow danced in the rain
with me and we laughed.
feeling whole on my own
is a memory I won't soon forget.

when you smile, you glow,
and make others around you glow, too.

it's exhausting to feel like you will never be good enough,
like you will never be happy in your own skin.
but I promise one day you will look back at how much
you've grown and be in awe of all the healing you've done.

you are healing. I can see it even if you can't. and you may be wondering why you still feel a bit hollow, why some days your chest still aches and tears spring to your eyes. each day that passes you are growing stronger, planting your feet more firmly on the ground. look at you go. be proud of how far you've come.

I hope for you
sunlight that stays,
that everyone you meet
smiles in your rays
without trying to take your warmth.

I hope you
never shiver,
never have to
search for a fireplace
in someone else's hands.

I hope you
never have days that
feel fragile,
like the earth could
shatter at any moment

and leave you the lone survivor.
you've been living
alone all this time. the world
should know by now
that you can handle it.

but I hope you won't have to much longer.

acknowledgments

infinite thank you's to my readers for supporting my books and helping me feel less alone. to the person reading this right now: *thank you*. I hope for you sunlight that stays, always.

to Michelle at Central Avenue Publishing: thank you for your support, and for giving this book a home among so many other talented poets!

to Beau, Jessica, and Molly: thank you for your feedback and edits to make this book the best it can be.

to Simon: my inspiration behind every happy poem. thank you for every day. I love you!

to my parents: thank you for your unwavering support always. I love you both.

to Theo: you were born the week I finished writing this book. I can't think of a better reminder to slow down and take in the magic of life. I love you!

to the poetry community: I'm inspired by your talent every day and grateful for the friendships I've formed with so many. thank you!

the poem titled *and for my next trick, anxiety doesn't live here anymore* came from a prompt by another talented Central Avenue poet, Raquel Franco.

Shelby Leigh is a bestselling author who explores mental health, self-love, and healing through poetry. She writes with the goal of making others feel less alone and to empower her readers to love who they are. When Leigh isn't writing, you can find her reading a good book, buying yellow decor, and/or probably eating chocolate.

You can find her at shelbyleigh.co